For all I know...to all my loved one's

TO: Loryn, Anton, Ludwig and Philipp - Thank you!

ISBN: 978-0-6454635-0-7 (print)

Print and Distribution Ingram (AUS / US/ UK /EUR)

NATIONAL
LIBRARY
OF AUSTRALIA

A catalogue record for this book is available from the National Library of Australia

A healthy dose of suspicion will shield
you from a great deal of stupidity.

⬦⬦⬦

A mix of skill and guts, with a bit of brains
thrown in, is a winning formula.

⬦⬦⬦

Adversity and hardship breed talent,
and develop and hone skills.

⬦⬦⬦

Adversity is merely a stumbling block
on the way to finding yourself.

⬦⬦⬦

A dvice is just another form of prose.

⬦⬦⬦

A fter shaking hands with the rich and powerful, make sure to wash yours properly.

⬦⬦⬦

A ll those who continually volunteer unsought advice and guidance evaporate mysteriously when things go awry – but never without declaring "I told you so" as they leave.

⬦⬦⬦

A lways aim for the impossible, otherwise even the possible becomes impossible.

⬦⬦⬦

Always be wary of business partners: they
are only as reliable and trustworthy
as the next opportunity permits.

∞∞

Always give more than you take.

∞∞

Always have a back-up plan – things
actually do go wrong.

∞∞

Always look beyond what you see and hear. It's
the hidden stuff that will knock you out.

∞∞

Always stay in touch and on good
terms with your enemies. One never
knows when one needs them.

∞∞

Always treat anything done selflessly for
the greater good and for humanity, and
anything done "for the people", with
contempt - until you are proved wrong.

∞∞

America seems like an overripe fruit someone
forgot to pick: hanging lonesome in a
tree, weather-damaged, picked at by
passing birds and full of worms.

∞∞

An ability to flick, swipe and search does
not make a subject-matter expert.

∞∞

Any kind of indebtedness clouds good judgement and erodes your independence.

~

As a rule, these are good starting points: it costs too much and the customer pays too little.

~

As I have grown older, a great deal of grey has crept into my kaleidoscope of colours.

~

As my friend says, "time is useless unless it is used".

~

As one grows older, diminishing senses make
good bedfellows – and can be liberating.

◇◇◇

As one grows older, one realizes that time
is a luxury one cannot get enough of.

◇◇◇

Asking is the cheapest form of learning.

◇◇◇

At times it feels like our societal policies are
made by prepubescent schoolchildren
for prepubescent schoolchildren.

◇◇◇

Average is an indication. Not a measure.

∞∞

Avoid asking for what you do not want.

∞∞

Be harder on yourself than on your fellow man.

∞∞

Be quirky. Quirkiness is sexy.
Quirkiness is power.

∞∞

Be very selective of who you let in – they
have a tendency to take over.

∞∞

Before asking, check whether you really
want to know the answer, and whether
the answer may complicate matters.

⊙⊙⊙⊙

Before being honest make sure
you can afford it.

⊙⊙⊙⊙

Before enjoying any proceeds from a last
will and testament, ensure there are no
handwritten notes hidden anywhere.

⊙⊙⊙⊙

Before you take your clothes off make certain
everything is impeccable. Once your
shortcomings are exposed there is no
dress large enough to cover them up.

⊙⊙⊙⊙

B eing a thief, one sees the thief
in everyone else.

∞∞

B eing friendly, helpful and forgiving
is normally interpreted as being
weak. It is not weak.

∞∞

B eing optimistic, there is hope that the
resurgence of totalitarianism will
highlight the dangers and risks to true
democracies – so that common sense
prevails, protecting and reinforcing
hard-earned gains and progress.

∞∞

B eing overly smart and intelligent
is not necessarily helpful.

∞∞

B eing too accommodating, and preoccupied
with policies catering to a few and those
on the fringe, compromises security
and prosperity, and paves the way for
ultra-conservative ideology and rules.

∞∞

B eware – not everyone is stupid!

∞∞

B eware of defenders and promoters of
medieval rules and practices.

∞∞

Beware of entitlements – they tend
to grow and take over.

∞∞

Beware of overcomplicating simple things and
simplifying things that require scrutiny.

∞∞

Beware when procedure matters
more than substance.

∞∞

Bordeaux, Burgundy, Lombardy, Rioja, Napa,
Barossa, Stellenbosch … contribute more
to a world of peace and harmony than any
religion ever has. Hands down. Any time.

∞∞

Brainpower on its own is useless. Passion
and patience, among other things,
are needed to make an impact.

∞∞

Brainwashing is a far more competitive and
widespread sport than football will ever be.

∞∞

Brilliance and above-average IQ guarantee
rational and responsible behaviour in
neither an individual nor a society.

∞∞

Building trust is a never-ending, monumental
task: no matter how strong the foundations,
it can be destroyed in a fleeting moment.

∞∞

By far the biggest and most frequent
form of prostitution has nothing
to do with sexual activity.

∞

"Calculated risk-taking" is an oxymoron.
"Using one's brain when making
decisions" is a better way to put it.

∞

Canonization and fake news
have a lot in common.

∞

Capitalising on victimhood does not work.

∞

Comfort is merely a breeding
ground for surprises.

◇◇◇◇

Comfort zones and tolerance work hand-
in-hand. The smaller the comfort
zone, the greater the tolerance.

◇◇◇◇

Complacency is an enemy in disguise.

◇◇◇◇

Complexity is not a pillar of stability.

◇◇◇◇

Computers have a very long memory
and tend to be antisocial.

∞∞

Convenience, like complacency, is
simply another form of credit
– it has a hidden cost.

∞∞

Decisions are there to be made. Not
too early. Not too late. On time.
And when no decision is needed
there is no need to make one.

∞∞

Delphic maxims: "know thyself – nothing in
excess – surety brings ruin" … Recite these
daily until they are engraved in your mind.

∞∞

Denying one's own hypocrisy is hypocritical.

⚬⚬⚬⚬

Desperation and jealousy are
traits to steer clear of.

⚬⚬⚬⚬

Dictators and revolutionaries spill their
own blood first. Initially, anyway.

⚬⚬⚬⚬

Dictatorship will never fall out of
fashion – it is too tempting.

⚬⚬⚬⚬

Do not mistake efficiency with speed of action. The faster one decides, the more one compromises efficiency.

∞∞

Do not owe anything to anyone, including yourself.

∞∞

Do not take advice from family or friends. Stick to people with experience in the subject.

∞∞

Do not volunteer information unnecessarily. No need to answer what has not been asked.

∞∞

Doesn't matter what people say – in the end they normally think you are stupid and treat you accordingly.

∞∞

Don't ask questions that cannot be answered truthfully and expect an honest answer. Few can afford to be honest. Few dare to be honest either.

∞∞

Don't forget – you and me are society!

∞∞

Don't let greed get the better of you. In the long run money means little – if you ever doubt this, speak to someone who is terminally ill.

∞∞

Don't let greed prevent you from
making sound decisions.

∞∞

Don't mistake your typical office environment
for a social-networking platform.
Especially when you are in charge of it.

∞∞

Don't shy away from asking for what is due
– especially when it comes to money.

∞∞

Embrace "couldn't be better" in all
walks of life. It's a philosophy
designed to help us cope.

∞∞

Ensure you protect your thoughts from racism and discriminatory, unjust ideas.

∞∞

Epochal change does not happen overnight.

∞∞

Even after a dictator has been disposed of, another is waiting round the corner to take their place.

∞∞

Every coach will confirm that unless you are hyped up you are not performing at your best.

∞∞

Every farmer knows that if you want to
make money you must get your produce
from the land, out of the ground,
off the trees and to the market on
time – otherwise it goes to waste.

∞∞

Every now and then, when I get the feeling
I am the only normal person around,
I stand in front of a mirror – voila!
I've doubled the number already.

∞∞

Every time misfortune strikes,
you are on your own.

∞∞

Fate is not something to tempt nor something
to choose – it is something to deal with.

∞∞

Feed someone honey long enough and
you end up with another queen bee.

∞∞

Fence-sitters, do-gooders, hangers-on
and their kind are plain, hopeless
irritants, of no use to you if you are
trying to make a difference.

∞∞

"For ever" is a nonsense phrase
– it doesn't exist.

∞∞

Forget about entitlements. There are none.

◦◦◦◦

Freedom starts by not owing
anything to anyone.

◦◦◦◦

Friendship and loyalty do not
mix well with business.

◦◦◦◦

Gandhi did not change the minds of
millions on one single train ride.

◦◦◦◦

Genuine enthusiasm always wins
the day. Every day.

◦◦◦◦

Get a sense of what people can
do and then halve it.

∞∞

Getting out of bed is merely the
first step in waking up.

∞∞

Greed is insatiable.

∞∞

Happiness is an acquired state.

∞∞

Hard work and self-confidence are
basic ingredients in most recipes.

∞∞

Have you ever seen what happens
to a "line drawn in sand"?

∞∞

Have you ever won an argument
with your spouse?

∞∞

Hiding the truth by not replying to or
sidestepping questions is like latent lying.

∞∞

History and experience hold water,
unlike assumptions.

∞∞

Hold your nerves. Control your
emotions. Stick to your line.
Being steady brings victory.

∞∞

Home is a powerful magnet.

∞∞

Honestly, how many real friends can one have?

∞∞

Honesty is a bit like playdough.

∞∞

Honesty is a very expensive virtue.
Unless you can afford it, you
may be better off without it.

∞∞

I am getting to that stage where one knows
more dead people than living ones.
Thinking about it, nothing's really changed.

∞∞

I don't know why men study when
women have all the answers.

∞∞

I've tried, but I cannot trace any
empire built on idle chatter.

∞∞

If it is part of your life, live it.

∞∞

If it needs 100%, then 99% is not enough.

oooo

If you are cocky and arrogant, make
sure you can back them up.

oooo

If you are on a mission, have a plan
and a road to travel on. Shut out
the noise and chatter. Focus.

oooo

If you are unwilling or too lazy to
make decisions, someone else
will make them for you.

oooo

If you blindly believe in faithfulness and loyalty, even with your most intimate, maybe you should get a dog.

∞

If you can read between the lines, hear what is not said and see what is not shown, then you are in a good spot!

∞

If you cannot maintain a healthy cash flow, then you'd better get a job. Preferably not in finance.

∞

If you do not have an answer, or a solution, shut up.

∞

If you do not like it, change it. If you cannot
change it, persevere with it until you can.

◇◇◇

If you have a basket full of eggs, invest in a
few more baskets but no more eggs.

◇◇◇

If you have to hit someone, hit them hard.

◇◇◇

If you make risky investments, stay focused,
sharpen your senses, remain engaged, and
watch out for enemies. Don't get hurt.

◇◇◇

If you mess up, face up – sort it out, there
and then. You'll sleep much better.

∞

If you run yourself down, you will be run down.

∞

If you see a train coming, get out of the way.

∞

If you think you can cruise through life
without experiencing at least one
major upheaval, think again.

∞

If you worked hard to arrive at a position,
defend it until you know better.

◇◇◇

Ignorance is a powerful weapon.

◇◇◇

Ignore any gurus who constantly
violate their own prescriptions.

◇◇◇

In a true circus there are no trapeze artists,
elephants or lions. Just clowns, lots of them.

◇◇◇

In business, the surest way to get it wrong
is to rely on what you are told.

∞

In business:
Rule #1: Nothing ever happens by itself.
Rule #2: Make sure something happens.

∞

In spite of my regimented upbringing,
today I can see beauty in chaos,
disorder and randomness.

∞

In the end you need to make a living
– preferably an honest one.

∞

Inaction and lack of urgency make
good bedfellows, and are poster
children for insomnia.

∞∞

Independently of your upbringing, whereabouts
and environment, there comes a stage
where you and only you control your life,
destiny, and – most of all – responsibilities.

∞∞

Irrespective of how honourable, principled
and genuine someone is, the surest way to
promote decay, erosion and contamination
is to elevate them to a position of power.

∞∞

It can get lonely on top and there is no shortage
of stormy days. But you see the sun rise
first, and can bask in it the longest.

∞∞

It is always easier to operate away
from the limelight.

∞∞

It is as important to know what one
has as what one does not have.

∞∞

It is not uncommon for people who focus on
winning the battle to forget about the war.

∞∞

It is very difficult to work with people
who never make mistakes, especially
when one is perfect oneself.

∞∞

It takes courage to be wrong from time to time.

∞∞

It was not the lack of talent that missed the
goal – it was the wrong boot, idiot!

∞∞

Judge yourself not on your successes, but on
the mistakes you could have avoided.

∞∞

Judging by what true capitalism does to some people, best stay away from it, for the good of yourself and those around you.

∞∞

Just because someone asks for an opinion doesn't mean they actually want it.

∞∞

Keep your highest highs and your lowest lows to yourself.

∞∞

Knowledge is power – train, re-train and keep on training.

∞∞

L earn to keep your thoughts to yourself.

∞∞

L earn to treasure your job. It's more
than most people have.

∞∞

L egacy is ego.

∞∞

L et the one causing bad news deal with
it. No need to volunteer to help.

∞∞

L ife is simple: no expectations,
no disappointments.

∞∞

L ife is worth living. Don't forget the living.

~~~

L ook after your money. Make sure it does
not end up in a bankrupt man's pocket.

~~~

L ook after, care for and tolerate your
immediate family. After all, that's the
only thing that counts in the end.

~~~

L oyalty has a price. Either way.

~~~

L uck is always on the side of the brave.

∞

M aintaining a healthy distance
means exactly what it says.

∞

M aking one's own problems someone
else's, while seemingly an art
form, is not a good practice.

∞

M any suffer from knowing too
much. Including me.

∞

M e, arrogant?! Must be folklore.

∞∞∞

M isfortune and loneliness have a lot in
common. So do luck and popularity.

∞∞∞

M istakes, errors and faults are quickly
apportioned to individuals. Success,
on the other hand, is owned by
an abundance of people.

∞∞∞

M odern life is all about taking and
siphoning off without contributing;
all about individual rights but never
about individual responsibilities.

∞∞∞

Money does not protect from
stupidity, nor disguise it.

❀

Never ask for favours, which can be costly. If
you really need something, buy it and pay
for it. Then at least you know what it cost.

❀

Never be sure of anything. Wait until the fat
lady has sung, and the money is in the
bank – and make sure the bank is safe.

❀

Never bite the hand that feeds you.
You always have a choice.

❀

Never forget or ignore data – it is truly
collectable, and it pays off at some stage.

◇◇◇

Never forget the arts – they can provide
great comfort when you need it most.

◇◇◇

Never temper with the right and privilege of
an old man's prerogative of being grumpy
and miserable. He may bite your head off.

◇◇◇

Never walk over dead bodies or kick someone
who is down and out. There is room
enough for everyone, and the way round
is easier, less hurtful and more human.

◇◇◇

No opinion, no point of view. No
discussion. No progress.

⬦⬦

No team that allows the slowest to dictate
the pace will ever win a race.

⬦⬦

Normally perception accounts for about
half, and deception for the rest.

⬦⬦

Not long ago the agenda was utopian,
then it was hedonistic. Now we
are in an age of self-entitlement,
preparing the ground for dystopias.

⬦⬦

Nothing is ever as addictive as freedom.

∞

Often, stepping back brings you closer.

∞

One of the fastest growing
weeds is entitlement.

∞

One way to waste time is to explain the
colours of a rainbow to someone
who does not want to see it.

∞

Only one thing must be protected
in business: cash flow.

∞∞

Only someone with a mind can
change their mind.

∞∞

Only the very last will counts.

∞∞

Only use friends if absolutely necessary.

∞∞

Others may think your pantry full, as long
as the expiry dates remain hidden.

∞∞

Overstaying one's welcome never
ends well. As they say, the fish
starts to smell after a while.

∞

Paranoia and gullibility create easy prey.

∞

Patience is underrated.

∞

People are strange. They prefer to go
with the flow rather than exercise
some thought. But they are quick to
complain when things go awry.

∞

People seldom help for no reason.

∞∞

Perception and deception are siblings.

∞∞

Please drink responsibly. Don't spill.

∞∞

Prudent paranoia is a good barometer. It saves
more lives than it ruins. Excessive paranoia,
however, ruins more lives than it saves.

∞∞

Remain principled, and redefine your
principles along the way. Grey areas
tend to grow, like weeds in grass.

∞∞

Remember – there may be no tomorrow.

~~~

Remember: Any debt, especially monetary debt, invites corruption and exploitation.

~~~

Remember: People vote with their feet every day. But at the ballot box only sporadically, if at all.

~~~

Remember: You are never as clever as you think you are.

~~~

Remember: you cannot overtake
at the same speed.

∞∞

Remember: Your blood is my blood.

∞∞

Respect and authority are earned.
Responsibility you are born with.

∞∞

Richness comes in many shapes and
forms – and often in disguise.

∞∞

Ride hard – there is plenty of rest ahead.

∞∞

Rules are meaningless if you
cannot enforce them.

∞∞

Rushed jobs and decisions tend to
come back and haunt you.

∞∞

Seize the moment – normally
you only die once.

∞∞

Self-deception should be classified as a drug.

⬦⬦⬦

Smart breaks and fortunes often come from luck and dubious characters. In the real world, hard, honest work and doing the right thing get you very far, and more than enough reward.

⬦⬦⬦

So far, I have not met a fainthearted leader. Nor have I met one with many friends.

⬦⬦⬦

Solidarity with one's own children is not necessarily a good thing.

⬦⬦⬦

Some make more mistakes than others.
Associate with the others.

∞∞

Some things cannot be pinpointed
to a particular time. They happen
seamlessly, like the change from
sexy underwear to bloomers.

∞∞

Sometimes one gets the feeling children are
running the show: the know-it-alls, over-
confident and on steroids … probably
because we encourage and enable them.
But it is The Sorcerer's Apprentice all over!

∞∞

Soon you too will be part of an age group
for whom mask wearing and daylight
curfews should be compulsory.

∞∞

Spoilt children seldom grow up.

∞∞

Standing still is never an option.

∞∞

Strangers seldom pose any danger. Beware
your close friends, your kin, your
family. Danger comes from within.

∞∞

Strength lies in unity.

∞∞

Subjectivity increases with experience,
learned behaviour and age, at
the expense of objectivity.

∞∞

Success breeds vanity, and eventually
vanity will take over, sooner or later,
if it wasn't excessive from the start.

∞∞

Success is very brittle, and unless it is
handled carefully it will not last long.

∞∞

Sugar-coating is a wonderful
and rewarding art.

∞∞

Surprise is the most important tool in the box.

∞∞

Survival lies in strength, not protection.

∞∞

Survival thrives on suspicion.

∞∞

Taste, good or bad, is largely a
function of income.

∞∞

That a hero never dies is not true. The lifespan of a hero is substantially below average life expectancy.

⬦⬦⬦⬦

The advances or failures attributed to a generation are really only the doings of the preceding one.

⬦⬦⬦⬦

The day you think you are smarter than the enemy, you have lost.

⬦⬦⬦⬦

The more complicated the structure the less money there is.

⬦⬦⬦⬦

The more fanatical, controlling and dominating a leader, the less they consider inclusiveness, and leadership, for all.

∞∞

The more people pretend, the less they have.

∞∞

The only qualities your foes find attractive are your weaknesses.

∞∞

The only way to deal with incompetence is to call it out before it manifests itself.

∞∞

The people who exploit you most are
usually the ones closest to you!

∞∞

The proverb "hunger is the best cook"
beats any motivational program,
any time, hands down.

∞∞

The relationship between patience
and age is inverse.

∞∞

The risk of promoting autocratic behaviour
is directly related to the proportion
of yea-sayers in the population.

∞∞

The softer and more accommodating the
policies, the sooner totalitarian rule sets in.

⬥

The struggle for life is won or lost
only on your deathbed.

⬥

There are always more opinions
than people in the room.

⬥

There are leaders and opinion polls.
Unfortunately there are more
opinion polls than leaders.

⬥

There is more than one opportunity
in life. Looking back they seem to
pop up in abundance: too many
to pay attention to them all.

∞

There is no pleasure in riding a wave
on someone else's misery.

∞

There is nothing convenient about truth.

∞

There is nothing like independence
– it simply does not exist.

∞

There is nothing wrong with being partisan.

∞∞

There is one way in life – like the progress
of time itself: forward and forward only.

∞∞

There should be no reason for doing
anything for no reason.

∞∞

Those with the least insight are
the most opinionated.

∞∞

Time is the ultimate luxury.

◇◇◇

Time is a great healer.

◇◇◇

To delay the onset of rot, things should
be shaken every so often.

◇◇◇

To keep dystopia at bay, societies
cannot rely on outside forces –
defence must come from within.

◇◇◇

To men: the sooner you use the
part of the body sitting above
shoulder height, the better.

∞∞

To truly appreciate and enjoy life, one must
first taste hardship, adversity and loneliness.

∞∞

Today's greed pales in comparison
with that of Louis the XIV and some
of his associates, both before and
after. We have come a long way.

∞∞

Too much confidence is bound to pop
like a balloon at some stage.

∞∞

Too often, telling is mistaken for asking.

∞∞

Treat time as an eternal enemy. It has a
tendency to throw the book at you
from nowhere, and you shouldn't be
surprised at how few pages are left.

∞∞

Treat work like it is the best medicine,
a miracle cure for most ills.

∞∞

Trust no one, not even yourself. Trust is
very expensive – like good advice.

∞∞

Trying is nothing to be ashamed of.

◇◇◇

Understand, forgive, tolerate –
but only up to a point.

◇◇◇

View what you face with a healthy dose of
suspicion – it makes for good judgement.

◇◇◇

Walking on the edge, or on thin
ice, sharpens one's senses.

◇◇◇

Wallowing in one's own misery
does not get you out of it.

∞∞

We are all hypocrites. Some of
us more so than others.

∞∞

We are bizarre. To become a saint
takes verification of two miracles,
but telling the truth and revealing
cover-ups are not among them.

∞∞

We are in a strange in-between stage as humans. We think we are advanced compared to our closest relatives, the primates. And while we are, when it matters most we follow our animal instincts rather than apply logic and wisdom.

∞∞

What is more pointed and honest than a fitting slang expression?

∞∞

What's your plan B?

∞∞

When dealing with people, don't let your expectations interfere with their ability and willingness to help.

∞∞

When facing adversity, toughen up.

∞

When going into negotiations weak, do
not expect to come out strong.

∞

When I was younger I believed in humankind
and fairies. Now I believe as much in
humankind as I believe in fairies.

∞

When marriage becomes a kindergarten and
a laundry, perhaps it is time for a change.

∞

When pleasing people, don't forget yourself.

⌘

When the act of eating has transcended
into an art form, while at the same
time the majority falls asleep hungry,
then it is time for a rethink.

⌘

When witnessing abuse, don't tolerate
it, no matter how inconvenient.
Otherwise it will haunt you.

⌘

When you are invited into a home, or a
country, never forget that you are a guest.

⌘

When you have planned well and think you
have everything covered – think again.

∞∞

When you're down and out, only one
person can get you back on your feet
and walking with pride again: you!

∞∞

Where there is money there is help.

∞∞

Where there is smoke there is often fire:
best to act first and ask questions
later, before it gets out of hand.

∞∞

Where there is wine there is hope.

⬦⬦⬦

Whilst the future might not be ours, it is up to us to make sure there is one.

⬦⬦⬦

Whilst the sky ought to be the limit, the reality is that most of us venture little beyond our comfort zone.

⬦⬦⬦

Who is Greta…?

⬦⬦⬦

Work is a privilege, not a curse.

⬦⬦⬦

You won't see how long the train is
by standing in front of it.

∞

Your biggest enemy is always you.

∞

Your destiny is in your own
hands, no one else's.

∞

Your goodwill in offering a little help
will be abused sooner or later.

∞

Your level of alertness and focus is directly
related to whether you are walking
the tightrope or simply practising.

∞

Youthful exuberance and confidence, mixed
with a healthy dose of experience and
maturity, and finished off with a sprinkle
of wisdom, make a powerful cocktail.

◇◇◇◇

Zweig, Roth, Rolland, Orwell... all people
I ought to have known 40 years ago.
Thanks Steve. Better late than never.

◇◇◇◇

www.ingramcontent.com/pod-product-compliance
Lightning Source LLC
Chambersburg PA
CBHW071851090426
42811CB00004B/558